Fragments of a Childhood

Paul Lindale

© 2023 by Paul Lindale
First Edition
Second Printing

All photographs © Peter Lindale except p.74, from *Picture Palaces of Liverpool* by Harold Ackroyd, and p.110, © Sharon LaBella-Lindale.

Book and cover design by Paul Lindale.

For my sister, Susan Lindale

Contents

	First Words	11
	Foreword	13
1.	I Am Born	15
2.	Memories, part one	17
3.	The Eagle Landed	19
4.	Winter	21
	On Tuebrook	23
5.	I Am the Baby	25
6.	Inside the Sweet Shop	27
7.	The Lucky-Bag	29
8.	The Butcher	31
9.	The Newsagent	33
10.	The Chippy	35
11.	The Waiting Room	37
12.	The Beggar	39
	In the Land of Nod	41
13.	The Cat and the Clock	43
14.	The Way Home	45
	Lost and Found	47
15.	Bullet on a Blue Day	49
16.	Hot Lead	51
17.	The Pound	53
	Fragments	55
18.	Champ	57
19.	First Drink	59
20.	On Holiday	61
21.	Sunburn	63
22.	Stuck in Traffic	65

23.	Night Lights	67
24.	Driving Home	69
25.	Unconscious	71
26.	The Hospital	73
27.	Diamonds Are Forever	75
28.	The Cinema	77
29.	First Match	79
30.	The Gutter	81
31.	Dad, part one	83
32.	Dad, part two	85
33.	Mum	87
34.	Nan	89
35.	Grandad	91
36.	Nitty Nora	93
37.	Tony	95
38.	The Idiot, part one	97
39.	The Idiot, part two	99
40.	The Magnifying Glass	101
41.	The Bully	103
42.	The Fly	105
43.	Bonfire Night	107
44.	Christmas Eve	109
45.	First Watch	111
46.	Dad's Bible	113
	Photographic Memories	115
47.	Gran	117
48.	The Girl in the Picture	119
49.	My First Car	121
50.	The Camera	123
51.	Teddy	125
52.	I Bleed	127
53.	Viva	129
54.	The Beer Bottle	131

	Final Words	133
55.	When I Was a Child	135
56.	Memories, part two	137
	About the Author	139

First Words

Foreword

Every childhood is personal; how can it not be? The experiences we accumulate along the road to adulthood become the lived memories we rely on as proof we were young, once upon a time. Of course, there are also the photographic evidence and passed-down family narratives which serve as reminders and fill in the gaps, but not all of those moments can be retrieved. Memory is, by its very nature, fragmentary.

At some point, all childhoods come to a gradual end. I believe my own childhood ended when I turned twelve, the year I started high school (or senior school, as it is known in the UK), and thus the works contained herein are based on memories of my experiences prior to that year. I am now 58, so many of those memories have been tarnished by time; one, I only learned several years ago, never happened at all.

I Am Born

I am born
In Wallasey,
Over the water,
Across the Mersey,
From Liverpool,
To loving parents

I am born
Kicking and screaming,
Bathed in blood,
On a damp December day
In the cold of winter

I am born
Helpless and innocent
Tabula rasa,
I remember nothing;
Remembering comes later…

Memories, part one

Memories fade and merge,
Tenuous fragments tumbling,
Creating new impressions in my mind:
Shadows,
Images,
Echoes,
Stitched and frayed,
Becoming a past unlived
Yet remembered;
A childhood now
My own.

The Eagle Landed

I am three and a half years old,
Watching the lunar landing
On the big black and white TV
In the living room,
My nose inches from the
Flickering screen,
My parents crowding behind me,
I see a blurry ladder and on it
A blurry spaceman
"One small step for man,"
Crackles a voice from the speaker...

Winter

Frosted panes
Above the sink;
A long icicle drips
Outside.

On Tuebrook

I Am the Baby

I am the baby
In the navy pram
Outside the sweet shop
Hands blue
Bathed in sunlight.

Inside the Sweet Shop

Inside the sweet shop
Row upon
Row upon
Row of glass jars of
Sweets of innumerable variety,
A spectrum of shape and color;
My head below
The glass countertop,
My hungry eyes scanning,
The empty scales awaiting
A child's careful choice.

The Lucky-Bag

The Lucky-Bag
Promised treasures
And offered disappointments-
You never knew,
But remained ever hopeful
The plain white paper bag
Contained unbridled joy.

The Butcher

The butcher
On the corner,
Filled with sounds of chopping,
Festooned with hanging carcasses
Marbled red,
Smelling fresh and meaty;
Blazing white ceramic,
Scales shining silver
In the sunlight.

The Newsagent

The newsagent
On the corner,
Home to comics
Filled with weekly tales of adventure;
My newsprint blackened fingers
Feverishly consuming page after page
In a relentless pursuit of *the end*,
Followed by a passionate longing for
Next week.

The Chippy

The chippy
Always in the evening
Lined to the door with
An expectant hungry queue
Eagerly awaiting their turn
Eyes scanning the offerings,
Scrawled in patient hand
High behind the counter,
Occasionally departing into the dusk
With a hot newsprint-wrapped bundle.

"Next!"
The frying sizzle of chips
And other tasty delights
Steak and kidney pies
Filling the oily air
Fat blistering sausages
With mouthwatering aromas.

"Next!"
Another happy patron accomplishes his mission,
The queue inches along
Drawing us closer to our goal,
Closer to the heat and busy cooks-
Chinese draped in white,
Efficient,
Emitting an abundance of salt and vinegar,
Wrapping paper parcels with practiced
Machine-like speed,
No movement superfluous.

"Next!"
My fingers grip the scratched stainless steel
Countertop sprinkled with salt,
Wet with vinegar.
"Two fish and chips please mate,"
says Dad.

The Waiting Room

The doctor's waiting room,
Forever stifling under the watchful orange gaze of
The electric heater,
Always filled with unhappy-looking people
Wrapped in heavy coats and scarves
Perched on the eclectic assortment of ancient chairs
Arranged along three walls;
An unidentifiable,
Almost unpleasant
But homey aroma
Filling the air
Like old age;
The threadbare rug covering the floor,
Ever the center of attention;
The occasional tick of the heater
The only sound daring to break
The hushed silence,
Counting down the minutes
Until the door to the inner sanctum opens
And someone's waiting
Will be over.

The Beggar

On a bench
Outside the church
On a cold
November night
Sitting next to my guy
Watching
The Tuebrook traffic go by
Waiting
For the next passerby
So I can beg,
"Penny for the guy!"

In the Land of Nod

The Cat and the Clock

From the ledge,
High above,
Came the mournful meows of
The black cat
Reverberating through
The encompassing shroud of
Darkness;
The gigantic gears of the clock
Looming behind the cat,
Spot-lit by an invisible source,
Grind away time
At an imperceptible rate.
"Meow," pleads the cat.
"Tock," intones the clock.
Far,
Far below,
My head rests
On a puffy pillow,
Dreaming eyes turned inward
To the strangely comforting scene
Above,
"Meow," longed the cat.
"Tock," assured the clock.

The Way Home

I made my way
Down Green Lane
Almost to the point
Where the school ended and
The houses began,
Feet seemingly dragging
Through treacle toffee,
Legs ignoring the forward thrust
Of my body,
Stuck in space and
Trapped in time
Like an exclamation mark
Like a paused VHS tape
Like a fly in jam.

I willed my legs to move and
I inched forward
A painful inch.

Sensing something behind me,
Daring no backward glance,
I concentrated on
My slow-motion progression;
Each inch feeling like
An hour,
Each foot a day,
I made my way
Down Green Lane.

Lost and Found

Bullet on a Blue Day

I found
The red encrusted rifle bullet
On a blue day
In the sun
On the beach,
Washed ashore on restless waves
By tide and
By time;
A rusted relic
Of some forgotten soldier
Of some forgotten battle
Of some forgotten war,
Never fired and
Never to be fired;
A young boy's pirate treasure,
Rare and precious,
Soon to be lost,
As the sun settled over the sea,
In the soft, dry sand
Of the dunes.

Hot Lead

Lying in the road,
Baking in the summer sun,
The lump of lead looked like
A dead grey bird,
Shot from the sky,
Hot, heavy, soft;
So soft I could
Fold it into new forms,
Form it into shapes,
Shape it into bullets,
Fire it from a gun.

The Pound

In a scrapyard
Along the dock road
Looking for Vauxhall parts
With Dad,
Rusting carcasses
Towering above us,
Around us,
Begging to be searched
For untold treasures,
I spied
With my little eye,
Hidden by the shadows
Beneath a car,
A green pound note,
Folded and creased,
Fragrant with oil,
Lost and now found.

Fragments

Champ

Dad stood in
The kitchen doorway
Beside the dog,
White gauze with
Red spot
Adorning its side
Where it was shot.

First Drink

One night,
Past my bedtime,
Dad came home
With lager and crisps
Cheese and onion,
Salt and vinegar.
Mum liked her lager with lime;
She gave me two sips
And I was on cloud nine.

On Holiday

On Holiday,
At Pontins,
Not far from the land of cheese,
In a dimly-lit circular ballroom,
Sitting at a circular table,
The aromatic aroma of
Alcohol on the air,
Dad arrived with a round of drinks
On a circular tray;
A dark-brown Shandy for me,
Disappointed,
Feeling left out,
Because I longed for the same
Rich amber,
Apple-infused,
Glowing liquid
As Mum and Dad had.

Sunburn

Lying on my belly
In the chalet
At night,
My sun-burnt back
Blistering bright red,
Watching a scary movie
Alone until
My parents came home,
I felt content.

Stuck in Traffic

Stuck in traffic
On a sweltering summer day,
Heat rising from the road
In shimmering waves,
Every surface scalding,
Dad's hands sweating
On the steering wheel,
A man emerges, barefoot,
Wearing only his undies,
From a car in the next lane
And dances and dives,
All elbows and knees,
Into the back seat,
To join a laughing woman
Dressed only in her underwear.
Dad shakes his head,
Unimpressed;
Mum giggles, says,
"State of him!"
I think nothing of it-
It *was* a hot day.

Night Lights

Driving home from Blackpool
At Christmastime
In the dark;
Me in the backseat
Sucking happily on a minty
Stick of pink rock,
Careful not to get
Sticky fingers,
Slowly honing an icicle point,
The illuminations file
Slowly by the windows
Filling the night with
Light and wonder.

Driving Home

Driving home from Southport
At dusk,
Shirley Bassey or
The Carpenters
Singing from
Dad's cassette player,
Reels rotating,
Softly clicking,
Nobody talking,
Tired from a hot day
In the sun,
On the beach.

Unconscious

Mr. Smith swiftly carries
My limp form in his arms
As I look down from above,
A watchful hawk
Riding the currents,
A sea of staring pupils
Parting before him,
Magnetized iron filings
Dividing the playground.
My stripey blue sweater
Dyed maroon,
Mr. Smith inserts fingers
Into my mouth,
Extracts something red,
Wet,
Glistening,
Flings it to the ground and
Heads towards the darkness
of the school entrance.

The Hospital

At the hospital,
After shot
After shot
After shot
After shot
After shot
After I wept
And cried, "No more!"
After the nurse cried in sympathy
After the head nurse briskly delivered
A final shot
After shooting the weeping nurse
A withering glance
After surgery
After I awoke to scouse for dinner,
I could not eat,
For my mouth had been
Sewn shut.

74

Diamonds Are Forever

When I was six
Dad declared,
"We're going to see
Diamonds Are Forever."
I didn't understand what that was
But it seemed like I should,
Like he expected me to;
So, we went,
Just Dad and I,
To a place I had never been before,
But would revisit many times,
To experience what I never had before,
But would again and again
With Dad.

The Cinema

Gilded art deco sconces,
Scarlet velvet curtains,
Smartly dressed ushers
Waving red-shaded flashlights,
Ladies bearing dimly-lit neck trays
Loaded with choc-ices
And other treats
Long forgotten;
People chatting excitedly,
Fading to a reverent hush
As the sconces dimmed,
The curtains parted,
The screen was revealed,
And the show started.

First Match

Evening,
On the green and cream bus,
Standing room only,
On the way home
From my first football match,
From Goodison Park,
Blue and white
Hats and scarves
Everywhere to be seen,
Standing next to Dad
"Two – nil," I said
In a quiet voice filled with
Pride and awe.
"That's right," said Dad.
"Two – nil," I repeated the score,
Satisfied,
Smiling a victor's smile,
The green and cream bus
Rumbled its way down
Tuebrook.

The Gutter

The piece of cast iron gutter
Fell from the roof,
Bouncing off Dad's head,
Sailing over the eight-foot brick wall
surrounding the yard,
Smashing the neighbor's kitchen window;
Dad's head needing stitching;
Me disbelieving.

Dad, part one

Dad,
With his four-inch finger NAILS
Forever tickling
Us laughing,
Screaming,
Crying,
Pleading
For him to stop;
Him growling,
Smiling with delight,
Convinced we enjoyed
His ministrations,
Until we eels
Wriggled free of his grasp,
Gasping for breath,
Slithered across the floor,
And lay panting,
Panting,
Panting…

Dad, part two

Dad,
With his course grit
Sandpaper chin
Constantly eroding
Our smooth cheeks,
Turning them,
Burning them
Bright red
As we screamed and
Yelled for him
To stop,
Stop,
Stop;
Him knowing better,
That "stop" meant "go,"
That red equaled green,
Continued his relentless
Pursuit of pain
Until our faces
Heated the room
And the house caught fire
And we lay listening
To our cheeks sing
Their furious song.

Mum

When Mum was thirty
She danced with me upon her feet.
Towering above me
She seemed so old,
Like the queen of all the world,
Her hair bound by
Clips and lacquer,
Smiling a youthful smile,
Me laughing with delight,
"Dee-dee, dee," she sang
As she danced with me upon her feet.

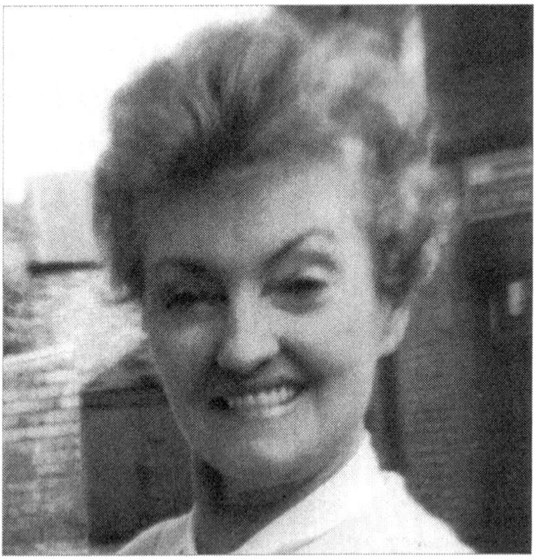

Nan

Nan would tell tales
Of her life in America,
Of working at Macy's on 5th Avenue,
Of being surrounded by sharks
Off the coast of Florida,
Of being caught in a multi-car
Pile-up on the freeway
(emerging quite unscathed),
Of uncle Eric helping save
The Apollo 13 astronauts.

She was never happy after
Her return to England:
She hated The Stranglers,
("That was not music")
The beef was too fatty,
Plates tasted of
Washing-up liquid;
Rats scurried through the walls
of her apartment,
People came in and stole things.

To escape,
She relived her memories
Of the good old days,
Of recharging batteries
With her bare hands,
Of couples making-out
On the back row
At the cinema,
The sound of garters
Snapping in the dark,
Making her smile
A young girl's smile:
Eyes alight,
Mouth open
In ageless wonder.

Grandad

We are visiting grandad
In the nursing home.
He is in his wheelchair,
Fingers stained
Nicotine yellow-brown,
Unsmiling,
Unhappy,
Unwell.

The afternoon sun shines,
Warming the gloomy interior
Of the common room.
I am drawing aliens
Assuring him they are real,
A babbling neophyte.
He seems unconvinced
Or else thinks me mad.
Unspeaking,
He stares into the past.

After he passes,
I inherit his gold signet ring,
Engraved with the sun,
Egg-shaped from
Snagging in his chair wheel.
Still wearable,
I wear it,
Treasure it,
Never reshape it,
Keeping him
And his chair
Close.

Nitty Nora

Nitty Nora
The hair explorer
Visited school,
Every once in a while,
With her special comb
She foraged
She searched
The locks of the girls and
The licks of the boys
For tiny infestations;
She pulled and
She tugged
Tears from our eyes
Until we emerged from the nurse's office
Abandon all hope ye who enter
Disheveled and tufted and
Dreading her return.
She had many faces,
All serious and severe,
But Nitty Nora
Was her name and
Hair her game.

Tony

"Tony is a boy's name,"
Chanted the playground urchins.
To which my amazon,
My benevolent Boudica,
Responded with a charge,
Fists and skirts flying,
Brown ponytail whipping
The air around her furious face,
Eyes full of brimstone,
Uttering a savage war cry,
Sending the fiends fleeing,
Shoes slapping stone,
Shrieks merging as one.

Tony stood smiling,
Breathing easily,
Hands at her sides,
Satisfied with the panic-stricken
Enemy's cowardly retreat;
Even now regrouping
At a respectful distance,
Possibly planning a repeat
Offensive.

Tony,
Who once saved me from the mob
On my birthday,
The first girl
I looked up to,
Admired,
Respected,
Feared
And loved
As only a boy of seven can
Love
A girl of eleven.

The Idiot, part one

The sky is bright blue
Wallpaper spread
Above my head,
So bright I squint,
Raise a hand,
Shadow my eyes,
As the stony tarmac
Burns into my back,
As I lie stiff,
Tensed,
In the road
Atop the hill
Listening carefully
Listening for
An approaching car.

The Idiot, part two

In the night
I see
The exposed innards
Of the streetlight
Nestled within
Their dark cavity:
Intestinal wires
Twisting,
Turning around
Metal organs
As alien as my own,
Begging to be examined,
Probed,
Touched,
I take up an implement,
Shiny and suited to the task,
Reaching out,
Making contact,
A steady stream of
Unfiltered power
Flowing through me
In a frozen moment,
Body vibrating,
Lit from within,
Skeleton
Silently
Screaming
Through a vice,
Until my friend
Shoves me,
Shaking still
Shaking,
Aside.

The Magnifying Glass

The sun shone
Through the glass,
Light honed to a
Bright white point,
Burning my skin.

The Bully

We stood by the streetlight,
My friend and I,
Watching
The bully in his puffy coat
Swagger down the street
Across from us.
We watched
As an alsatian turned the corner
Leading the slim, tall Pakistani,
Whose family owned
The corner-shop.
We watched
As the boy and his dog and
The bully in his puffy coat
Walked and swaggered
Towards each other,
Each seeing the other,
Alsatian ears alert.
We watched
As they drew alongside each other,
Glances exchanged like tokens.
We watched
As the dog sensed something,
Some mean streak,
Some hidden hostility
Towards its master,
Growl,
Rear,
Turn and tear into
The back of the bully,
All jaws and claws.
We watched, terrified
As the bully screamed
In fear,
In fright,
In pain,
As the beast shredded

His puffy coat and slim back.
We watched
As the boy regained control of
The still snarling. salivating
Monster,
Elongated fangs
Huge and white
In the moonlight.
We watched
As the bully slowly regained his feet,
Legs trembling,
Body shaking,
Creature's bloodlust subsiding.
We watched
As the bully shambled,
Sobbing,
To the street corner and then
Was gone,
Sobs slowly fading into the night.

The Fly

Earl and Birdy
Sat behind us on the bus.
Earl caught a bluebottle and
Proceeded to pull off its wings
One by one.
He let the fly,
Which could no longer fly,
Walk aimlessly along
The top of the seat back.
He laughed
Until he grew bored,
Then again picked up
The pitiful creature and
Proceeded to pull off its legs
One by one
Like flower petals,
(*She loves me,*
she loves me not)
Until there remained
Only one.
Earl and Birdy laughed and
Laughed at the immobile
One-legged fly
Until,
Teary-eyed,
Earl abruptly grabbed Birdy's thumb
And,
As I watched aghast,
Squashed the ghastly remnant flat,
Red juices squirting,
As Birdy cried out
As I gagged
As Earl laughed even harder
As the fly,
Which was no longer a fly,
Wept in silence
And the bus lurched on.

Bonfire Night

Bonfire Night
In Newsham Park,
Fireworks rocketing
Into the winter sky,
Filling the darkness
With sparkles and explosions
Of color and light,
Zipping,
Whistling,
Crackling like gunfire,
The crowd emitting
Ooh's and ah's of awe,
The acrid odor of
Gunpowder and smoke
Wafting on the wind,
The guy burning
Atop the bonfire,
Alone.

Christmas Eve

Christmas Eve,
Lying awake in bed
Pretending to be asleep
Trying not to fall asleep
Waiting for Mum
Or Dad
To come stealthily in
Bearing the black bin bag
Full of toys
To lay quietly
At the foot of the bed
And then creep away
Into the night and
Their own waiting bed.
Only then could I let go of
My tenuous hold on
Wakefulness and proceed into
The Land of Nod.

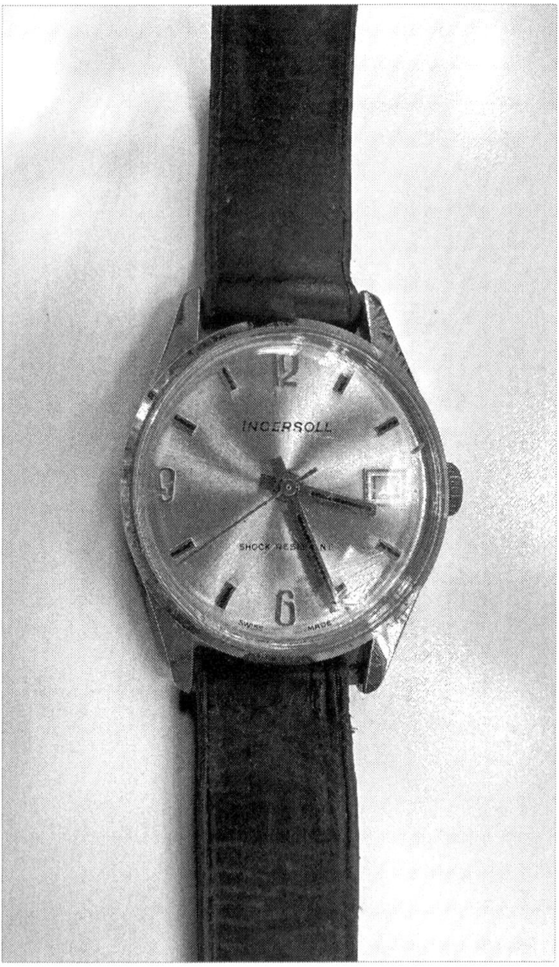
INGERSOLL

First Watch

Tick,
Tick,
Tick,
Sings the smooth Swiss mechanism
Beneath the shiny silver facade
Beneath the gleaming crystal
Tick,
Tick,
Tick,
Hands sweep through
Their imperceptible
Individual arcs
Tracing time:
Tick
Seconds becoming
Tick
Minutes becoming
Tick
Hours in
Endless circular cycles
Day becoming night
Becoming day;
Future becoming
Present becoming
Past in an instant
Tick,
I watch my childhood
Tick by…

Dad's Bible

Dad's burgundy,
Bonded leather bible,
Worn cover closed,
Sat on his white bedside table;
Red silk ribbon,
Protruding near the spine,
Twisted and curled,
Marking his place;
Worn gilded pages waiting
To be turned,
For the Word of God
To be opened.

Photographic Memories

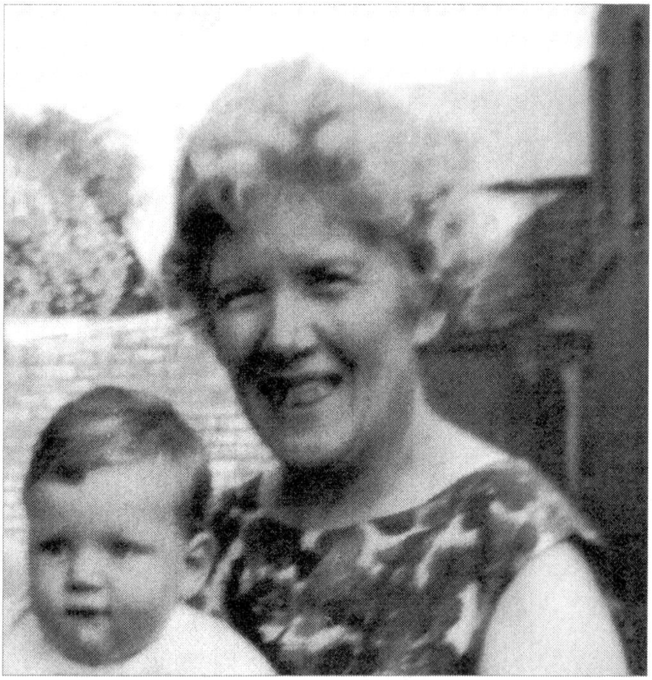

Gran

In the photograph
Gran is holding baby me,
Smiling,
She seems happy.
She was mum's mum and
I do not remember
Her touch,
Her smell,
Her voice,
Her laugh;
I do not remember her name.
Cancer took her.
Now,
There is only
The photograph.

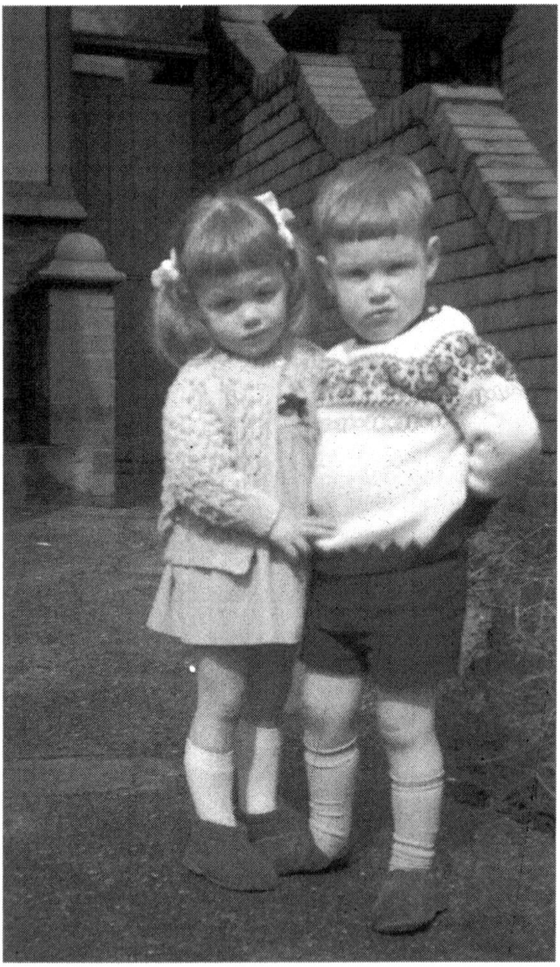

The Girl in the Picture

In the photograph
I am standing next to a
Blue-eyed, blonde
Girl;
Let's call her *Dorothy*.
We are about the
Same age
Same height
Both wear red slippers,
White socks;
Mine dirtier,
More masculine.
We seem unhappy
With our arranged
Marriage-playdate,
Weary of our time together.
Dorothy touches my sweater
With two fingers
Meaning
She is with me,
For better or worse;
We are an old couple,
Older than our parents,
Stuck in time.
Did Dorothy click her heels,
Disappear?
I do not remember,
There is only
The photograph.

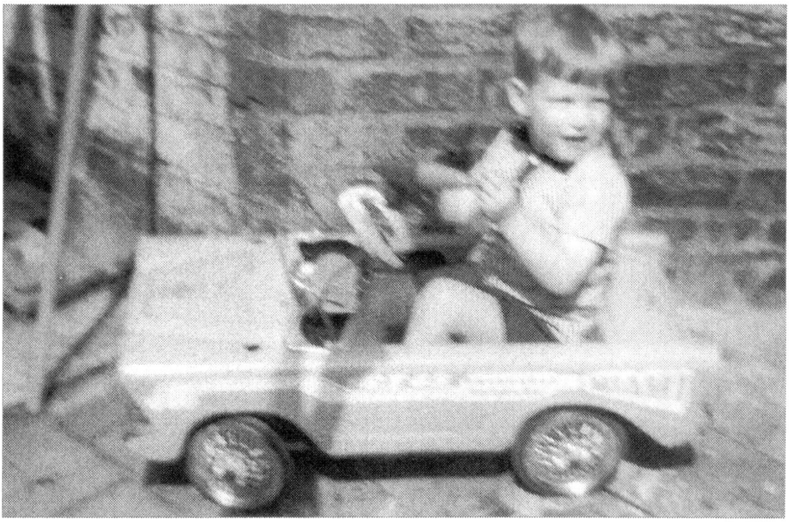

My First Car

In the photograph
I am sitting in a blue metal car,
Room for one only.
The sun is shining,
I am smiling
A joyous smile.
My parents say
I loved that car;
I do not remember,
There is only
The photograph.

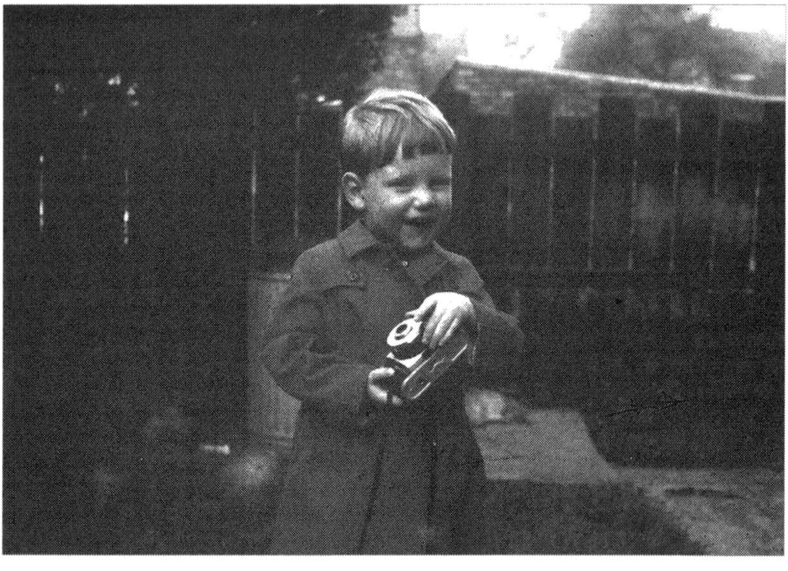

The Camera

In the photograph
I am holding a camera,
Wearing a navy blue
Mackintosh with many pockets,
Smiling,
Happy.
My parents say
I never went anywhere,
Rain or shine,
Without that coat;
I do not remember,
There is only
The photograph.

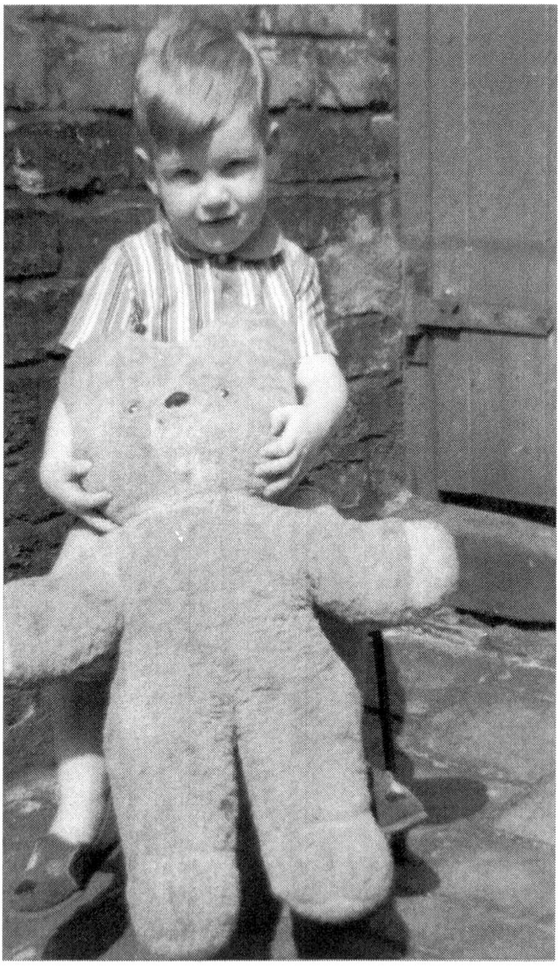

Teddy

In the photograph
I am standing before a door
In the front room
Or
Outside of the house,
Holding a yellow-orange,
Straw-filled bear before me.
The bear reaches my chin,
Will share my bed,
A source of comfort,
Until the age of rebellion,
When he will become filler
For a punching bag.

I call him *Teddy*
For that is what he is
And all he can ever be.

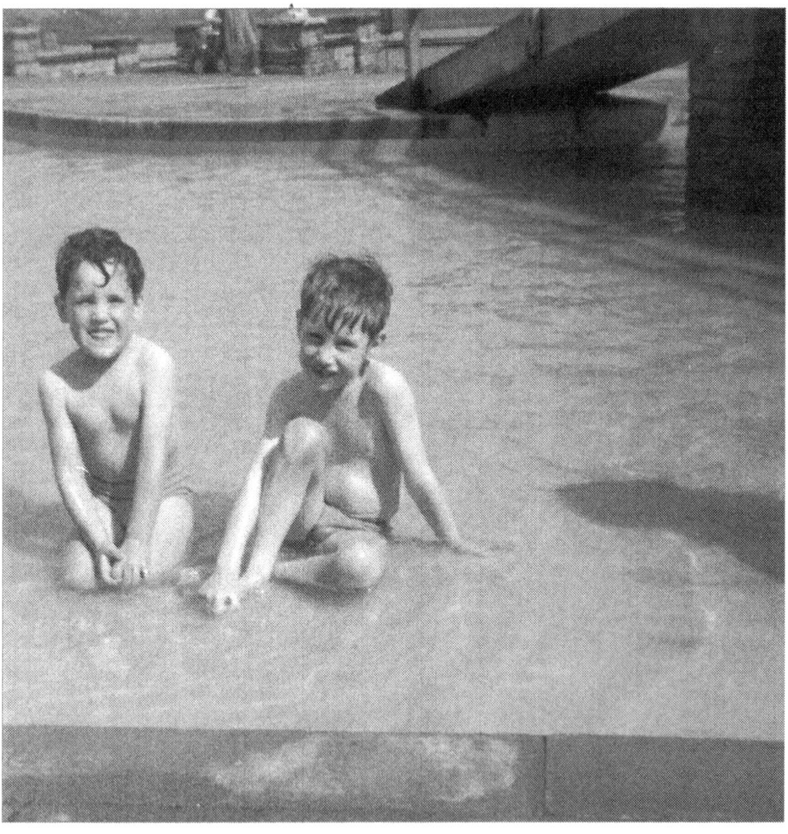

I Bleed

In the photograph
I am sitting with my brother
In a shallow pool
Lined with lumpy blue paint.
We smile for dad,
Forever behind
His Kodak Instamatic.
I grip my foot tightly,
Blood seeping unseen
Between my fingers
Into the cool water.

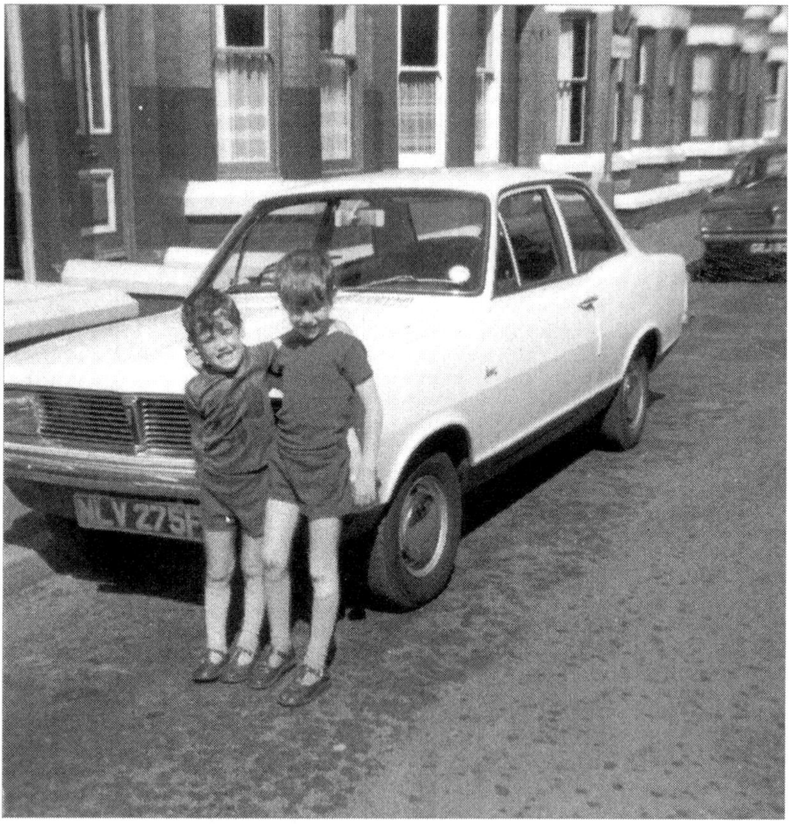

Viva

In the photograph
I am posing with my brother
In front of Dad's white Vauxhall Viva
(was it new?)
We are dressed all in blue,
As all boys are,
Arms around each other,
Smiling,
He pulling away,
Eyes closed,
My finger in his ear.
I do not remember this moment,
There is only
The photograph.

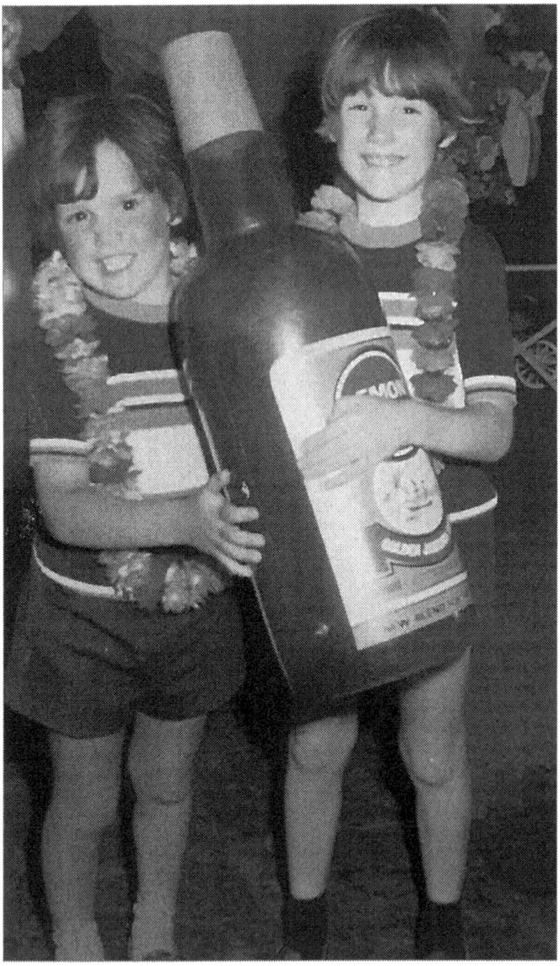

The Beer Bottle

In the photograph
I am standing beside my brother
On the dancefloor
Brandishing a big brown
Plastic bottle of beer,
Bigger,
In memory,
Than both us boys,
We grin and bear it,
Flash-frozen
For the briefest blink
Of an eye.

Final Words

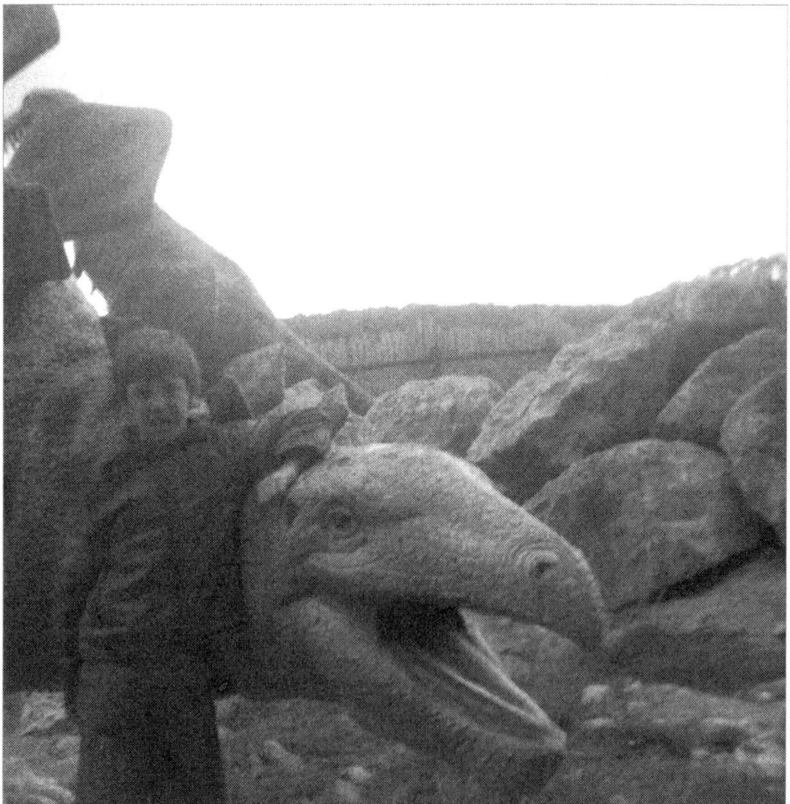

When I Was a Child

When I was a child,
I dreamed of being
An archaeologist,
Of digging up dinosaur bones
In the desert.
On Sunday mornings
I drew at mum's dresser:
Tyrannosaurus
Brontosaurus
Stegosaurus
Triceratops,
My mind feverishly fueled by
Books and movies.

An archaeologist,
I never became,
But still I draw
And am drawn.

Memories, part two

These fragments wash up
Along the uncertain shore
Of my mind,
Shimmering in the sun
Before being swept away
Into the deep darkness
Beneath the waves of
Memory's turbulent tides;
Eventually resurfacing,
Faded and worn,
Blurred by the filter of
Time.

About the Author

Born 1965 in Wallasey, Merseyside, England. Paul Lindale is a visual artist, designer, and educator. Lindale has exhibited throughout Massachusetts and in Texas in the US, and in Liverpool and London in the UK. He taught at Massachusetts College of Art & Design and Westfield State University from 1993-99, and was a full-time professor at Greenfield Community College, MA from 1999-2023. He currently resides in Northfield, Massachusetts.

Fragments of a Childhood is Paul Lindale's first collection of writing.

Printed in Great Britain
by Amazon